Scholastic CLIFFORD THE BIG RED DOG™

Phonics Fun
Reading Program
Book 4: e, ee

Clifford and the Bees

by Janelle Cherrington
Illustrated by Josie Yee

Based on the books by Norman Bridwell

SCHOLASTIC INC.
New York Toronto London Auckland Sydney
Mexico City New Delhi Hong Kong Buenos Aires

Clifford, Cleo, and T-Bone play hide-and-seek.

Clifford is It.

He does not peek.

Clifford looks.

"I see Cleo!" he says.
"She is in the weeds."

Clifford looks.

"I see T-Bone!" he says.
"T-Bone is near
that tree."

Clifford looks up.

"And I see bees!" he says. "T-Bone, look out!"

T-Bone looks up.

He sees a big beehive—
and lots and lots of bees.

T-Bone jumps to his
feet and runs!

HELP US

But the bees do not
fly near him.

They keep to one spot.

"Look," says Clifford.
"The bees seem to
be spelling!"

Clifford looks.

He sees that part of the tree is weak.

Clifford tells the bees, "Come with me."

Yum—a sweet treat
to eat!